Winning by GIVING

WITHDRAWN

Written by Nancy Kelly Allen

Content Consultant
Taylor K. Barton, LPC
School Counselor

rourkeeducationalmedia.com

Scan for Related Titles
and Teacher Resources

www.rourkeeducationalmedia.com

PHOTO CREDITS: Cover: © Ariel Skelley; page 4: © MoniqueRodriguez; page 5: © GYI NSEA; page 6: © Clerkenwell_ Images; page 7: © artpipi; page 8: © Kondoros Éva Katalin; page 9: © Stígur Karlsson; page 10, 17: © fstop123; page 11: © mangostock; page 12: © auremar; page 13: Dragon Images; page 14: © LifesizeImages; page 15: © Catalin Petolea; page 16: © Adam Kazmierski; page 19: © Daniel Loiselle; page 21: © Jani Bryson, © Catherine Yeulet; page 22: © mangostock

Edited by Precious McKenzie

Cover and Interior Design by Tara Raymo

Library of Congress PCN Data

Winning By Giving / Nancy Kelly Allen
(Social Skills)
ISBN 978-1-62169-910-1 (hard cover) (alk. paper)
ISBN 978-1-62169-805-0 (soft cover)
ISBN 978-1-62717-016-1 (e-Book)
Library of Congress Control Number: 2013937305

Rourke Educational Media
Printed in the United States of America,
North Mankato, Minnesota

Also Available as:

Educational Media

rourkeeducationalmedia.com

customersevice@rourkeeducationalmedia.com • PO Box 643328 Vero Beach, Florida 32964

TABLE OF CONTENTS

EVERYONE WINS

Everyone needs help sometimes. Helping others is called **philanthropy**. You can give time, work, or money to someone who needs it. That's a way to show people or causes they are important to you.

There are many ways to get involved in community service. If you are interested in construction, try volunteering with an organization, such as Habitat for Humanity.

People want to be treated fairly. Having the same number of turns in a game is fair to all. Share and be fair. You'll have fun and win friends, too.

Who can help others? You can!

Begin by helping your friends. Everyone needs a friend. Friends **share** things. They listen to each other and make each other feel good. They work together and play together. Sometimes friends put the needs of others before their own because they care.

As you get older, pass along toys you no longer play with. You've cleaned out your closet and someone else has a new toy. Everyone wins!

DONATION

THE POWER OF KINDNESS

Sometimes people get upset. These are important times to help. Listening to a friend who is upset is a way to offer **kindness**.

A kind word is like dropping a pebble into the water. The pebble makes a splash. The splash makes ripples that spread. A kind word can send ripples of joy and comfort to someone who is having a rough day.

A smile might be the perfect gift to make a person feel better.

Your smile can have the ripple effect and make others smile.

Giving clothes is another way to show kindness. Pass down clothes that no longer fit you to younger family members and friends. Or, you can **donate** your clothes to thrift shops or homeless shelters. This not only saves money, but keeps the clothes out of landfills. When you reduce trash you save energy.

Give clothes and shoes that are in good condition to people who need them. Your old coat could keep someone warm in winter or dry on a rainy day.

COAT DRIVE

VOLUNTEER

Tap into your **talents** to help others. Do you like to cook? How about cooking a meal or a simple dish for your grandparents? Homemade biscuits and a pot of soup is delicious and nutritious. Your grandparents would really appreciate it!

Decorating a school for a dance or painting a park bench can be exciting for those who like art. If you like to sew, making a cloth doll for a child in a homeless shelter would be a special gift.

Do you love sports? You can share the fun by assisting with a team of young players. You'll be a hero in their eyes. Or, you may prefer tutoring. Some students struggle with math and reading. Your talents and efforts can help a child succeed.

SMALL THINGS MAKE A BIG DIFFERENCE

Every day, every home has lots of jobs that need to be done. Setting the table and taking out the trash are daily **chores**. These chores are easier if all family members lend a hand. Helping your family shows you care about them. It will give you a good feeling, too.

Encourage your family to work together on a project. You can spend time together as you rake the neighbor's lawn. Lending a hand can make a big difference in people's lives.

FOLLOW THE GOLDEN RULE

Treat others the way you want to be treated.

School offers many ways to give to others. Pay attention to students who are bullied. Stand up for your friends, even when others tease or laugh at them. Maybe someone will stand up for you someday.

Show a new student around the school or sit with that student at lunch. Give some of your time to the student and make a new friend. After all, wouldn't you like it if someone did the same for you?

THE HABIT OF GIVING

Giving is a **habit** you can do every day. Praise friends and give compliments when they do well. Celebrate their good times. Let them know you are happy for them, and thank them when they help you. Friends will celebrate your good times, too.

Birthdays and holidays are times to party and receive gifts. We often ask, "What are you getting?" These are also times to think about how thankful we are for what we have. Get into the habit of asking, "What am I thankful for?"

When you have a birthday party, instead of getting gifts, ask your friends to donate to one of your favorite charities.

Go green! Being green means caring for the environment. A work party with friends is a fun way to pick up trash in a park or along a stream. Recycle the bottles, paper, and cans. Everyone wins. The community is cleaner, and **volunteers** enjoy giving back to the community they love.

Joining a club is a great way to work on a project to help your community. You might learn to sew or build a doghouse. You can use these skills throughout life. Many community clubs are all about learning and helping others.

CAN YOU THINK OF OTHER WAYS YOU WILL WIN BY GIVING?

- COLLECT FOOD FOR A LOCAL FOOD BANK
- PLANT TREES FOR THE ARBOR DAY FOUNDATION
- VOLUNTEER FOR HABITAT FOR HUMANITY
- WORK IN A COMMUNITY GARDEN
- VOLUNTEER TO READ AT YOUR LOCAL LIBRARY

Help plant a community garden. Volunteers can share the food. Some people may donate the food to families that do not have fresh vegetables to eat.

Do you enjoy being outdoors? Walking a neighbor's dog or cleaning a nature trail may be jobs that fit you. Your work and time can make a difference.

HAVE FUN HELPING

National Volunteer Day is the Saturday before Thanksgiving.

When you volunteer you are making a choice to improve your community and the lives of others. Have fun giving your time, talent, and treasures to make the world a better place. Small acts of kindness add up to big results. As you can see, there are many ways you can help. Good citizens help each other. They are winning by giving!

GLOSSARY

chores (CHORZ): jobs that you have around the house

community service (kuh-MYOO-ni-tee SUR-vis): voluntary work to help others in your city or town

donate (DOH-nate): to give as a gift

encourage (en-KUR-ij): to give help or hope

habit (HAB-it): a regular behavior

kindness (KINDE-nis): to be friendly and helpful

philanthropy (fuh-LAN-thruh-pee): giving time, work, or money to someone who needs it

share (SHAIR): to divide something between two or more people

talents (TAL-uhntz): natural abilities

volunteers (vah-luhn-TEERZ): people who do a job without pay

INDEX

WEBSITES TO VISIT

www.kidsface.org/pages/thefacts.html

www.more4kids.info/704/top-10-recycling-websites-for-kids

www.pbskids.org/itsmylife/friends/bullies

ABOUT THE AUTHOR

Nancy Kelly Allen lives in Hazard, Kentucky, with her husband. Nancy loves to read, and her local library loans her lots and lots of books. She also loves to read books she has written to the kids at the library. Everyone is winning by giving.

Meet The Author!
www.meetREMauthors.com